Think Big Marketing for Small Businesses

Targeted Promotions for Success

By Kirby Hasseman

PublishAmerica
Baltimore

© 2009 by Kirby Hasseman.

All rights reserved. No part of this book may be reproduced, stored in a retrieval system or transmitted in any form or by any means without the prior written permission of the publishers, except by a reviewer who may quote brief passages in a review to be printed in a newspaper, magazine or journal.

First printing

PublishAmerica has allowed this work to remain exactly as the author intended, verbatim, without editorial input.

ISBN: 978-1-61546-385-5 (softcover)
ISBN: 978-1-4489-8565-4 (hardcover)
PUBLISHED BY PUBLISHAMERICA, LLLP
www.publishamerica.com
Baltimore

Printed in the United States of America

Dedication

For Amy, Skylar and Jade…you are the reasons I strive to succeed. Thank you for the inspiration. I love you.

Acknowledgments

As I consider all of the people I need to acknowledge for patiently teaching me through my career, the task seems too daunting to complete.

First, thanks to my dad, my first and best advertising teacher. He and my mother showed me early on that we can accomplish those things we set our minds too.

Also, thank you to all of those dedicated targeted marketing professionals involved in ASI and PPAI. Much of what we discuss in these pages are topics you suggest each day.

Specifically, thank you to the hard working professionals at Halo/Lee Wayne Corporation. My peers there have taught me a great deal about how to best make customers a success! Thank you to all of you…and stay targeted!

Think Big Introduction

Let's face it. If you are a small business owner then you are busy!

You probably hear other small business owners say all the time, "I don't have time to (fill in the blank). I have to manage employees, handle customers, stay on top of inventory, keep control of the books, sell products, service customers, return calls, and more! I don't have time to go home! I certainly don't have time for a book!"

But you know differently! By picking up this book you show that you understand that there are certain things you have to invest in your business (and in yourself) other than money. So you have **made** time. But this book is not about time management. It's about thinking BIG for your small business by utilizing **targeted** marketing strategies for big returns.

So since we know you are busy, we have made this book an easy to digest "magazine-style" read. You can come to it when you have time…and refer to it as you need.

There are so many aspects that you need to keep on top of when it comes to properly marketing a small business for growth. So we will touch on those in some detail in each chapter. But if you need to simply review a chapter or two as you get ready to launch a new product line, we feel like this format will allow you to do that with the most effective use of your time.

In addition, we will sprinkle in some real-life case studies to articulate how these concepts do work for business owners around the country. Because when you decide to invest yourself into a book like this one, you want to make sure your ROI (Return on Investment) is as possible.

So in keeping with the theme of brevity…let's get started Thinking Big!

Think Big Basics

If you really want to think big for your small business, then you have to master the small details first. So this chapter will discuss the basics of creating your Think Big Marketing Plan.

For some of you, this will be sort of elementary stuff…but it's important. And even if you feel like you have all of "the basics" down, I usually find value in reviewing them. If you are like me then you know the basics, but find yourself getting away from them in the daily grind of running a company. It's easy to do!

So let's start with the basics to make sure the business is on solid footing before we get customers beating down our door!

Know Who You Are

I know this might sound elementary but you would be surprised at how many companies that don't really know who they are. This is not just a question of company culture, though that is a part of it. It goes to the basic question of what you are selling and how much you want to charge for it! In addition, you need to know who might actually pay for this product or services.

Once you have the "who you are" message wrapped up in a bow (and many of you already do) then you need to outline your strengths and weaknesses. What can you do better than the competition? What sets you apart?

It's not just important to list the strengths (though that might be the most fun!) but you need to really know your weaknesses too. It will not only allow you to consider ways to improve the business, but will also help you keep in mind what services and products NOT to market. Because of course there is no reason to drive customers to your door if you can't fulfill on the promise. They won't come back!

Consider this your company's SWOT analysis. A SWOT analysis is where you analyze your company's Strengths, Weaknesses, Opportunities, and Threats. This exercise can be invaluable as you consider what direction to take your business. And it can also serve a truly valuable service when you consider what you want to market…and how to do it!

Know Your Customer

Once you have a stronghold on who you are, it's time to sit down and envision your perfect customer. Who are you selling too? What do they look like? What do they like to do? What are their interests? What do their friends look like? This is vital information to understand when you being to create your Think Big Marketing Plan. It will allow you to understand what media to focus on…and what to avoid completely as a waste of money!

Create the Business Plan

If you have been reading the previous paragraphs and thought, "But isn't this covered in my business plan?" then you are probably right. But there are two problems with that assumption: 1) Many companies don't have a viable business plan and 2) those who do haven't seen it for LONG time! As we begin to think about how to better market your business, now is a time to Create (or RE-create) your Business Plan.

Many business owners I know think that this is an exercise to be done only when the bank needs it. And though I certainly will concede this is not the activity I want to be doing on a Saturday night, it's a vital thing to check off your to do list. If nothing else, the business plan forces you to answer questions about things that will determine your success as a company. If you need a template for a business plan then we can provide one at the end of the book. It might feel time consuming, but it can mean the difference between success or failure in a business life (or a marketing campaign).

If you spend a few hours working on it, it might save you thousands of dollars. That is a wage per hour that I can handle!

Finding Your USP

When I work with businesses about creating their Think Big Marketing Plan I always ask them "What is your USP?" Those who can rattle it off without explanation are almost always a step ahead of those who stare at me with a look of befuddlement.

For those who fall into the latter category, your USP is your Unique Selling Proposition. This is the exciting story you tell potential clients about the magical reasons why to do business with you...and no one else. Your USP is what sets you apart from your competition and makes you the only choice for your customer.

So what is our USP? Are you the fastest delivery service in town? Are you the least expensive jeweler? What is it that differentiates you from the pack? If you don't know, then your potential customers won't know (or care) either!

Take a few minutes and write down your USP so that you can recite it when someone asks you "Why should I do business with you?" I can't think of a more important question you should be able to answer on the spot!

Elevator Speech

Okay...you have your USP and you know how to use it! (Sounds kinda dirty doesn't it?). Now you need to be able to tell that story without boring the daylights out of someone. The concept with the Elevator Speech is: you need to be able to share your USP with a client on the ride up the elevator. After the doors open you lose them. So now that you have your USP work to condense it so that you can tell it in no more than 30 seconds. If you can't do that...you will lose a lot of potential customers.

Whittle it down until you can make your elevator speech in 30 seconds or less. And just think, if you can do that it just might come in handy later (when writing scripts for radio and TV!).

Okay…so those are the basics. As I mentioned, some of you might have found that to be review; but it never hurts to review. So let's make sure we have our foundation strong by polishing off our business plan, fine-tuning our USP and Elevator Speech, and let's move on to Thinking Big!

Review: The Basics of Marketing Your Company
1. Know Who You Are
2. Know Your Customer
3. Create Your Business Plan (or revisit it to make sure it is on track).
4. Create Your USP!
5. Create Your Elevator Speech!

Developing the Think Big Marketing Plan

"I want to market my company, but I don't know where to start!" There are an enormous amount of options when it comes to marketing your small business, and those options seem to explode exponentially as the days go by. So where do we start?

Well…with a plan!

So many businesses today take the approach that they can "throw a bunch of stuff at the wall and see what sticks." Though that certainly is an option, it's a very easy way to waste money. In addition, it makes it nearly impossible to track any results in an intelligent way. So businesses (not yours of course!) find themselves at the end of the month with less cash flow that they expected…and nothing to show for it!

I think we can all agree, that is NOT Thinking Big…and NOT targeted! So we will show you how to improve your marketing returns by using **targeted** marketing strategies!

Lay Out Your Weapons

When I am creating a marketing plan for myself or one of my clients, I like to take a look at ALL of my options in the area. I make a list of all of them so that I can consider them as I consider the budget and the plan. That way, if I get a call after the plan has been implemented I can honestly say that I considered them…but have decided to allocate marketing dollars elsewhere.

This is not to say you can't change plans. But if you have taken the time to consider these options, you are less likely to spend your marketing dollars (or worse your profit) on a whim!

I consider this like laying out my weapons. Once I have them all out on the table I can decide what best will help me win my customers!

Know Your Area

As you "lay out your weapons" it is important to know your area. If your area has a dominating TV station then you need to consider that as one of your main "weapons." Businesses in my area have had a great deal of success with radio because there is one dominant station that produces results. It is important to know what works in your area as you allocate your marketing dollars.

If you don't know the answers to these questions, don't be afraid to ask. If you are comfortable with asking competitors, then give them a call. But more than likely you can glean the information from other small businesses that have common customers.

Don't be afraid to ask them what works best for them…and what doesn't work! More often than not, they will be MORE than willing to tell you! I have found that when it comes to advertising, small businesses are very willing to share their successes and their disappointments.

CASE STUDY

A great example of a client of mine that knows his market is Jeff Drennen. Jeff owns several car dealerships in different areas…and he knows how to market! In his first market, radio was king. So Jeff spent a great deal of his time and energy working the radio station to his great benefit. He did 60 second ads and 30 second ads. He sponsored football broadcasts and even had a Saturday morning high school football program at the dealership…every Saturday!

This was no small investment…but his results were huge. He took a flailing car dealership and made it the powerhouse in the community. How? He did it by knowing what worked in that community. He understood that with only one radio station in the area, this mass media outlet was very targeted when it came to his specific audience.

Then he purchased two dealerships in another neighboring community. Though the new dealership was not that far away, the balance of power in the media changed, and Jeff changed with it. He still spent dollars on radio, he shifted the bulk of his investment to television with great results. Jeff's face (and the face of his son) became very well known in the area. So did his slogan, "When you are thinking of buying a new car, it's time to talk to Jeff!"

Jeff could not have had his level of success without great service, products, and knowing his USP. But the BIG lesson here is that Jeff knew his market and what media would work best to sell his company!

Figure Out the Numbers
Now is when we need to sit down and be a little bit realistic. Take a look at the numbers you can realistically spend in the first six months. It's great to have the huge dreams about Super Bowl ads, but this is where the rubber meets the road.

You have taken the time to lay out all of the options for marketing your company at this point…so you are ready.

What I like to do is create a paper with the months all laid out. This allows me to create my base plan, but then factor in the seasonal sales, promotions, product launches, etc. so that I can look at the whole year at once. That way if we decide to go all out and spend more on one month, we can do so while keeping an eye on the whole year's numbers.

Once you have the basic numbers laid out on the table (this is just a starting point number) now you can use your knowledge of the area to create your consistent marketing base. This is the way you are going to get in front of your customers with the most consistency.

The example above (with Jeff Drennen) showed how a company can use radio or TV to consistently be in front of their potential customers each day, but there are certainly other ways to reach your targeted base. My company, for example, is not prone to mass advertising. We utilize other promotional options to be our consistent image in front of clients. You need to choose your best option based on your knowledge of your area…and your clients!

This base marketing message is crucial to creating a consistent brand in front of your customers each and every day. And it is my belief that you need to give this option at least 6 months before you can dismiss its results (or lack thereof). So many times clients try something for one month and then want to move on to something else. At that point you have not given it a chance to break through. If you get results faster than that…great! But if you are not willing to give a campaign 6 months, then in all likelihood you should not do it at all!

Create Your Big Theme!

Okay. You have created your monthly plan of what you will spend. You have decided what media you will use to get that message across. You have the skeleton of your campaign. This is not the sexy part of the campaign, but by doing these things are you are far ahead of many small businesses. Now let's get to the fun stuff.

This is the time to get creative by looking at your USP, your message, and your budget and create your own marketing theme.

Roll up your sleeves…get out paper and pencil…open a bottle of wine (or whatever)…and start writing down your ideas on paper! Write down every idea that pops into your head. Put down ideas about your TV spots (if you choose do them). What is the theme? What will it sound like? Write down overall campaigns…what will be your slogan? What message will you leave with your customers? Write it all down…because you will be going back over it later!

Now is when you can begin to create your advertising "brand" so don't think any idea is too hokey or stupid. If it is, you will figure that out later. But make sure you get all of the ideas on paper. I have had some luck doing this in a group. As ideas start to flow, one will build upon the other and soon you won't be able to write them down fast enough! It's a fun and exciting process!

Now that you have filled up a piece of paper (or several pieces) with your ideas, it's time to edit. Depending on how long you've been at it (or how many glasses of wine) sometimes it is better to sleep on it. Come back to the ideas with fresh eyes. Now you can see which ideas are pretty hokey...and which ones still sound good! If they still sound good to you after 24 hours, you might have a winner!

I also like to run these ideas by a completely objective bystander or two as well. This will tell you if the brilliant concept you have in your head translates to someone else.

Also, keep in mind that the idea of your advertising is to sell your product or services. Often we get so caught up in the idea or concept that we forget to sell! Make sure your concept still ties back to creating a demand for your company!

Putting It All Together!

Now that you have your theme, go back to your numbers sheet and see how you can best "tell your story." You might re-think the media you are using...or you might be right on. But it is important that you maintain your theme or your brand as you move forward. So make sure you choose your advertising venues with your new campaign in mind!

Now make it happen! You have created a well thought out and (hopefully) creative marketing campaign for your business! Congratulations! Now commit to it and give it time to create results! Good luck!

Review: Creating Your Marketing Campaign
1. Lay out your marketing weapons (keeping your own area in mind).
2. Figure out your budget (so you know what dollars you have to work with).
3. Create your Marketing Theme!
4. Put the pieces together!

Big Marketing with Press Releases!

From the perspective of the small business there are few things more underutilized than public relations. By simply taking the opportunity to send in press releases, you will be ahead of 90% of small businesses I see.

And what a shame! Because of all the tools you have at your disposal (all of the weapons based on Chapter 2), public relations can not only be the most powerful...but the least expensive!

I am continually amazed at small businesses who tell me they "don't have time" to create press releases. Let me tell you my friends...make time! If you don't have time for free advertising that has more credibility than your paid advertising, then close up shop! You obviously are not in business to make money! If you are interested in sticking around, however, let's talk about press releases!

Press Releases

One of the easiest and most affordable ways to promote your business is simply by sending press releases to local media. Of course when you do this, it is completely up to the news editors as to whether these press releases ever see the light of day, but it's a numbers game.

Send the release to as many appropriate media outlets as you can...and send them as often as you can. If any of them take...you have a home run! Not only will they often give you exposure, many viewers/readers will feel it is more credible...**because it's not an ad**! In addition, I always recommend sending a picture (when sending to print). If they run the picture with the press release it radically enhances the amount of eyeballs that will check it out!

Getting the Press Releases In

So you've spent the time to create the press release, but how do you get them to run it? Of course there's no guarantee, but here are some things you can do to tip the scale in your favor.

1. Call the news outlet to discuss the press release in advance. Ask questions about how they like to receive them (email? Fax?). Ask what their deadlines are for getting them on to the air or in print. Find out if there is a specific person that handles your type of business news.

2. Format them professionally. If you want the news organization to take you seriously, take the time to make your release look professional. Don't just type your release in an email (though that can work after you have a relationship with folks). Take the time to formalize the process by using a form that I will put at the end of this chapter.

3. Include your contact information. Rarely will they contact you with questions, but make sure they can if they need too.

4. Give them the headline in Bold Capital letters. Don't make them guess what it's about.

5. Let them know the release date. Most of mine are for Immediate Release, but make sure that is clear.

6. Write it like a news story! Format the press release like stories you see in the newspaper or on the news. If you make it really easy to run your release, the likelihood increases that they will. They are just like everyone else…if yours is easy to use and another one they have to work at…guess which one they will use?

7. Add a quote! This is just my own philosophy, but I always have a quote. I do this for two reasons. 1) If they leave it in, I have made it look even more like a news story, giving it even more credibility. 2) If they feel like they "have" to edit something (and sometimes they feel like they should), then this is the easy place for them to cut. That way they leave all of the pertinent details in!

8. Submit a picture! As I mentioned earlier, this is a fantastic way to spice up your press release and ensure more eyeballs to check it out.

9. Wrap it up with contact information. Give the reader of the press release information on where to contact your business, find more information, or purchase your product or service.

Okay…so you have the basics! So what are you waiting for? Obviously you want utilize press releases to promote any new event, product launch, training completion or company milestone. But make sure you take *every* opportunity to send in a press release. I often joke about *creating* reasons to send in releases. Of course you want to be ethical, but you will find that once you start looking, there are lots of reasons to promote your business!

So get started today! Think about why you can send in a release to your local paper, radio station, or magazine. Below you will find a mock-up of a simple press release you can use!

303 S. 4th Street
Coshocton, OH 43812
(740) 622-7429
kirby@hassemanmarketing.com

FOR IMMEDIATE RELEASE

KIRBY HASSEMAN PUBLISHES MARKETING BOOK!

Coshocton, OH—Kirby Hasseman, owner of marketing and advertising company Hasseman Marketing & Communications, has published a new book called Think Big For Small Businesses! / *Targeted Marketing For Small Businesses*. Hasseman created the book in order to be a tool for small business owners to grow their business through exceptional marketing efforts!

Hasseman has been working with small businesses to help them create a buzz with their marketing for nearly 10 years. His simple, no-nonsense marketing approach helps businesses maximize their exposure while keeping their budget in check.

"I love helping small businesses reach their potential," says Hasseman. "This project will allow me to help more businesses be successful!"

In addition to the book, Hasseman has created a new website to help small businesses as well. There you can sign up for a free eNewsletter, read articles and posts by the author, and get great marketing ideas. The site can be found at www.thinkbigsmallbiz.com

To purchase Think Big For Small Business, you can visit local bookstores or www.thinkbigsmallbiz.com

-end-

Think Big with Video

One of the most effective ways I have found to promote your business is through video marketing. As technology advances, it is also becoming a more cost-effective way to promote as well. Now video marketing can mean several different things, and we will do our best to explain them, and talk about what might be best for your business.

Have a Vision for Your Production

Regardless of the way you choose to "broadcast" your video marketing, it is very important to have a well-defined vision for what you want to accomplish with your video. Now I am not suggesting you have each shot, angle, lighting, etc. planned out—that's the video production company's job to do—but you can certainly save everyone time and money by explaining exactly what you want (and sometimes *don't* want!).

In order to really have this vision, you will need to make sure you have the basics down (see chapter 1). Make sure you have your slogan, message, image, and brand nailed down, even before you have the scripting begun. In addition, for those clients that want me to write their scripts for them (and many do) I really appreciate those that can help with the basic direction, phrases, and tone they want to communicate. Let's face it: no one knows your business like you do. So if you choose to have someone else do scripting for you, make sure it sounds like *your* business…not like every other one!

But make sure this vision comes (with some discussion with its feasibility with the production company) BEFORE the production begins! You can save yourself hundreds (if not thousands) by making sure that your vision is feasible and affordable in advance. Each of those re-edits (or even re-shoots) cost a great deal and can make a project much more than you have budgeted. So do what you can to get everything done in as short a time as possible.

If you know what you want, and plan it out, most productions can be done in a day or two tops!

Using Faces to Sell You!

I am a big believer in making your video marketing piece very personal by using faces. This is a pretty simple strategy that accomplishes a few things in one fell swoop.

First of all (and maybe most importantly) having a face on the TV is very likely to catch a viewers attention. People are naturally attracted to the faces of people. And of course if you can get them to begin watching your marketing video, then all you have to do is keep them! You are half way there.

Another reason to use faces is that it will personalize the product or service you offer. Let's face it: people do business with people they like. So by portraying a likeable, personal image, it gives people another reason (other than needing your product) to give you a call!

Tell the Story with Video

Now this may sound a bit redundant when it comes to marketing with video, but you would be surprised how many businesses miss this mark. Marketing with video is a VISUAL medium that also has sound. It is NOT a radio ad that also has visual elements. It's a small differentiation with big results. Think about what your potential clients or customers will see…not just hear. I actually tell my clients that we should be able to watch the video (commercial or whatever) with the sound off…and have it still be effective. So when you watching your promotional video, put on your customer eyeglasses and make sure you understand what you are selling…and what they need to do to get it! Don't make it a mystery.

I think too many times we get hung up on making a promotional video (i.e. a commercial for television) funny or cute and we lose sight of the goal…to sell your company. There is nothing wrong with using humor or creativity in your video presentation (in fact I love it!) but don't forget this is a marketing tool first. If you make the audience laugh but they don't remember you...what's the point?

Use Testmonials to Tell the Story

Since you know I like using faces to the market, you won't be surprised to hear that I like using testimonials when appropriate. There is just nothing more powerful than a paying customer touting your service. It has credibility. Done right, this customer can tell your story better than you...because they (in theory) have no vested interest in blowing smoke! Obviously, they need to be well-spoken and articulate, but this can be the best story telling device you have.

Don't be afraid to ask your best customers to help you with testimonials. And this is not exclusive to video. When sending mailings to potential new clients I always include testimonial letters from excited customers. Use it to make your video presentation big!

CASE STUDY

Echoing Hills Village is a non-profit organization that works with individuals with disabilities. They are a faith-based ministry that has long term healthcare facilities around the state of Ohio. They also do camps and other services as well. We were working on a video project to show to potential donors. The idea of the video was to tell the story of how this organization touches the lives of those it serves. So we interviewed family members of the individuals. Not only did we showcase the impact the organization had on the individuals, but also their families.

The interviews were extremely compelling. Echoing Hills had done a great job of selecting the family members...and their testimonials were powerful. When the project was complete there was discussion of adding more shots to "speed up the pace" of the video. Though I understood their desire to move the pacing along, I convinced them to leave it alone and show it as it was.

The results were huge! When the president of Echoing Hills Village came back from the first presentation he thanked me. There wasn't a dry eye in the house. The testimonials were so powerful that we didn't need to do anything else! For more information on Echoing Hills Village you can visit them online at www.echoinghillsvillage.org.

Keep It Simple…Keep It Short

Nearly every other day I have a client tell me something like this: "I want to do a 20 minute video to promote my (fill in the blank.)" And my answer to them is always the same. "No you don't. Not if you want anyone to watch it!"

Customer's attention spans are remarkably short. Though you might be able to watch, listen and even talk about your business for hours on end (and you should…hopefully it's your passion!)…no one else really cares that much. So cut to the chase and keep it simple for the viewer. When you are working in the parameters of broadcast, there are some boundaries that are built in (i.e. 30 second spots, 60 second spots, etc.). But even then, I too often see businesses try to jam 45 seconds of material into 30 seconds. It's just inefficient and cumbersome. No one will remember it all…so why bother?

In addition, when creating that overall marketing video for your company keep those time limits in mind as well. I usually recommend 3 to 5 minutes as an optimal length for a video. There are occasions when a longer video presentation is called for, but it better be damn good if you plan on anyone getting through the whole thing. People often think that they sit through 1 hour programs all of the time on television—but they don't. They usually sit through 5-7 minute programs with commercial breaks in between. These lengths give a person a chance to take a mental (and bathroom) break in between viewing. In addition, these programs are often based on enormous budgets, professional screenwriters, stunts, visual effects and more…do you have that budget? If so, please give me a call! I am glad to help clients burn through money unnecessarily!

Remember, this rule is up to you most of the time to abide by. Unless you have a very honest video production house, they will gladly take your money. And the production will probably be awesome. But at then end of the day the success of a video is measured by whether or not the phone rings. So don't get too caught up in all the "cool" effects if they don't help meet that end goal. And besides, if you can get the same results from a $4,000 video (rather than a $20,000 video) then why not help your bottom line?

We will discuss the details of where to "broadcast" your video in the next chapter. But keep these principles of video marketing in mind when creating your next BIG promotional video!

Where to Utilize Your Video Marketing

In my experience clients go into a video project with a sort of narrow and singular focus. That's a mistake. A large portion of your budget with any video project (though certainly not all of it) goes to getting a camera crew of appropriate size out to a location to your company's shoot. If they are doing it right, they will have cameras and microphones, lights, tripods, etc. All of this takes billable time and manpower.

So why go to all that trouble to only shoot ONE thing? Going back to my point about planning out your video project, make sure you consider all of the alternatives to showing this project that you are going to pour a great deal of money into! In other words, make sure you THINK BIG!

What do I mean? Well, let's consider some of (not all of) the options!

Cable TV Advertising

One of the most cost effective ways to promote your small business through video is now through ads on cable TV. These are a great (relatively) low cost way to get out to the masses. But in order to maintain your "targeted" approach you need to carefully select the channels on which you will air your broadcast gem. Work with the sales rep to figure out where your business *needs* to be. Make them show you demographics and facts and figures to back up their assertions. But you can reach a nice audience with a limited TV budget on cable.

Another random thought about cable advertising: I would not have them produce the spots. Though some cable production houses are great, many are just thrown together in order to make cheap spots to put on the air. You don't want a "cheap" spot;here, like everywhere else, you get what you pay for. And it limits the flexibility you will have with other video marketing options!

Using Video with Direct Mail

If you plan the video project properly on the front end, you will hopefully have an extended "commercial" to use for other purposes. Once you have the video completed to your satisfaction, then the options open up!

For example, we spend a lot of time on direct mail in another chapter, but video can be an extremely effective way to market through the mail. By putting your short video on a DVD or USB drive, you create a cool marketing piece that can be used extremely efficiently as a mailer. If you can create a short, effective video and get it in the hands of your target customers, then this video can turn your order conversion rate through the roof! Consider this statistic: A Harvard Business School study reveals that people remember 20 % of what they hear, 30% of what they see, and a whole 70% of what they hear AND see! So getting a video in the hands of your targeted customers can be an awesome tool!

Make sure you consider packaging when sending a video through the mail. As with other direct mail, your success can be determined when the targeted customer looks at it initially. If it creates excitement, interest, and curiosity on the outside, then you are light years ahead of getting them to look at the video on the inside!

CASE STUDY

Ravens Glenn Winery in Ohio opened their doors around the same time I began my video production business. The owner, Bob Guilliams, and I met in his newly opened Wine Tasting Room and discussed the idea of using video to show off his wonderful facility. Bob and I shared the vision of creating a video that was not only beautiful, but short. He knew that he would only have his target's attention for a short window, so we decided to tell his story quickly.

Once the video was completed, I agreed to let Bob duplicate the video on his own in order to save his costs. Then Bob and his team mailed out this video to hundreds (if not thousands) of group tour planners around the country.

The results were huge. Ravens Glenn Winery grew into one of the best known wineries in Ohio. Though the mailed video was not the only piece in his marketing weaponry, it was an effective, targeted tool that was a huge part of his success! If you would like more information about Ravens Glenn Winery (and you should!) you can find them online at www.ravensglenn.com.

Using Video on the Internet

Another fantastic way to share your video with the public is on your website. Again, brevity is the key word here. With video on your website you can tell your USP to a clientele that is seeking you out for more information! You can use the video on your site to tell your story, encourage them to sign up for your mailing list (or email list), or even nudge them to action for the purchasing mode!

The fact is, the shift of emphasis for many forms of advertising today is to drive traffic to your website, rather than get them to make a purchase. Why? Though of course you want them to purchase from you, by driving them to your site you can accomplish so much more! You can get them to sign up for an eNewsletter, show them additional products that they might be interested in, capture their mailing information AND get them to purchase! It's not just one purchase you are after. You want to capture a customer for life!

With the video on your site, use it to drive them to sign up for newsletters and become that customer for life. Some really effective sites that utilize video often have several short video pieces for different purposes on different pages. Have a video welcome piece. Have a piece that tells the story of what makes you different. Even have a special video that explains your process or product and why you are the best! Be creative! But keep it brief!

Utilizing Video with Email

Though often it is easier and more efficient right now to use email to send a link to your site (where a video awaits), the day is coming when you will be able to embed video right in the body of an email. The files are getting smaller and more compressed so that emailing them is becoming possible. When that is a real possibility, then it will open a new marketing door that I will be excited to go through!

Right now, many great email marketers embed images in their email with great success. And as you move toward the time when you can embed video safety and efficiently, it will be a home run! But since we aren't there quite yet, attaching video as a file is appropriate in some instances. And again, if you can tell your message quickly then this might be a great tool for you!

Video on Other Internet Sites

I can hear some of you saying, "What about YouTube and other sites like that? Of course you should utilize sites like that…what are you out? (For those that don't know, YouTube.com is a website that you can load your own video on for free. It's easy to do and they have a huge audience).

The only thing I caution here is that unless you have a REALLY unique product or video, it can easily get lost on this huge site. That being said, it is an easy way to load your video for the world to see. And once you have it on YouTube, it is pretty easy to load it onto other websites as well! Oh…and if you do happen to have a video that becomes "viral" on a site like this, be ready to replace the phone lines because you are about to become a millionaire!

Using Your Video at Speaking Engagements

Another way I see video utilized well is when people use them in front of live audiences. Sometimes a well-constructed video can do a better, more concise job of telling the company story than a live speaker. In addition, it can break up the monotony of a speaker too. Remember, we humans have very short attention spans, so the more you can break up a presentation the more you can keep the audience engaged!

And not to beat a dead horse, but brevity will serve you well here too. A smart marketer will do a quick introduction and break the ice with the audience. Then they can move to the appropriate video for support. Then when the audience is impressed with the company and what you to offer, you bring back the live speaker to wrap it up and answer their questions!

And frankly this is just the tip of the iceberg. Once you have a properly thought out and constructed video, you can use it is a lot of ways to promote your company. Have your video promoting you at Trade Shows, Career Fairs, and any other place you are addressing the public. But just make sure you are always on the lookout for another way to use it. The best video in the world will do you absolutely no good sitting on your desk! So let your video do your company's selling even when you are not able too!

Big Marketing with Promotional Products

Since this book is dedicated to targeted marketing ideas in order to make a big impact, this chapter is a BIG one! Utilizing promotional products to market your business can be one of the most cost-effective and *targeted* ways to reach your customers…again and again.

"Wait a minute," you say. "How does my business handing out pens make a big impact on my overall brand?" And if you are simply handing out pens with your name on it, frankly it might not. But let's assume you have utilized promotional products sporadically with just that idea in mind. You still have done your business a service. Though you really should be thinking it out more than this (if you want to be truly targeted), consider this.

What is the worst thing that can happen to that pen when you hand it out with your information on it? Your prospect or client might look at it…see your name…and then throw it away. Bummer, huh? You have just "wasted" $.50. Well then, consider that this is probably the best-case scenario for nearly any other advertising medium. If your potential customer hears your ad on the radio—and it registers—it's a success!

Now realize that the vast majority of recipients of your $.50 pen will not throw it away. They will use it again and again. And then if they lose it or leave it someplace else, it leaves a whole new prospect to see your message too. Now that is one well spent half dollar! And in reality, based on this example, you hadn't even considered why you were handing it out…or who you were giving it to. If you add a more well-considered plan to these promotional pieces, your impact will be even larger.

Stay in Front of Clients All Year

What if you could spend $10 per quarter on your very best customers (the 20% that is responsible for 80% of your business) in order to thank them for doing business with you? No problem. What if in addition to that "thank you" perception, that $10 kept you in front of your customers all year long? Seems like a no-brainer when broken down like that, huh? Well, that is exactly what the right promotional product campaign can do for your company!

When I meet with new clients to discuss their promotional needs, I first talk with them about building their "foundation" for their marketing campaigns. This "foundation" consists of items that will stay in front of clients all year long. These items have a very low "cost per impression."

The cost per impression (CPI) is calculated by dividing the cost of the item by the number of times a customer will actually see your advertising message. For example, if you spent $20 on a promotional watch for your top clients, then the cost per impression would be figured by calculating the number of times that client would look at a watch and see your advertising message. The average person looks at their watch approximately twice per hour and we will be conservative by saying only 10 hours a day. Assuming the watch lasted a year (based on only 300 days) then you are looking at 6000 "impressions." Wow! Now divide the cost of the watch ($20) by the 6000 times the customer looked at the message and you come up with $.003333. Now that $20 gift becomes a very affordable marketing campaign. Factor in the fact that this message goes ONLY to where you want, and it becomes even more exciting!

So we consider these low CPI items when we build the foundation of their marketing campaign. So what are these magic promotional items that last a long time and keep our marketing message with them? Ironically, these are often the items some clients feel are less exciting. Examples of some great items with a low CPI are mousepads, notecubes, watches, magnets, and of course, calendars. Each industry is different and there are some great items with low CPI for each industry. Just consider where your clients or customers spend their time, and figure out what product can be there all the time!

Calendars…Your Silent Sales Person

At the end of the day, you want your advertising dollars to be as effective as possible…that's the point of this book. So I would be remiss if I didn't spend just a moment on calendar advertising.

If you are already on board with calendar advertising, then this might remind you why. But if you are not a believer, just give me a minute on this. Calendars are the ultimate in targeted promotional advertising. Obviously they (by their very nature) spend 24 hours a day, 365 days a week on the wall, on the desk, in the home, even in the pocket of your customer. They are always there…your silent sales person.

Consider this…85% of all people who have a calendar on their wall know exactly who gave it to them. And of those, 95% do business with that person! There are no "gimmies" in advertising, but utilizing calendar advertising as one of your "foundation" items is close. And let's put it to the CPI test! The average person looks at their calendar 10 times a day, 350 days a year. Go ahead…do the math.

In addition, a nice calendar can either accompany or be your year end gift to your clients. It's a nice marketing touch to thank them for their business anyway, so why not have something that will remind them of you all year long?

Obviously you need to spend a bit of time considering what kind of calendar to hand out (there are a lot to choose from). You know your clientele, so you need to consider what they would like to receive. In addition, make sure it is a theme you can be comfortable with as representing your company's brand. And of course…you can always do a completely custom calendar. The price for printing one has come down considerably in the last 10 years.

Build the Theme with Promotional Products in Mind!

As you are creating your marketing campaign for the year or the quarter, it's important to consider how to tie in a promotional item to add lasting power to your campaign. I am not suggesting that you only utilize promotional items to market your business. I am, however, suggesting that you can add impact and longevity to the overall campaign by doing so effectively.

If you are a furniture store having a sale, then consider handing out measuring tapes to clients so they can measure their living room and see what furniture will fit! A new car dealership could hand out a road side safety kit for any new car purchase. A new coffee shop could purchase imprinted travel mugs for those that want to take their great coffee on the go. There are limitless ways to build your brand through promotional items. But it's important to think it out and create a well-thought out marketing piece.

Regardless of the campaign, there is a way to increase it's effectiveness by adding a well thought out promotional item to the mix!

CASE STUDY

A magazine wanted to increase their distribution through gaining more paid subscriptions. Two revenue sources would increase if they could get their circulation up by 5%. First they could charge more to advertisers by bringing in a higher circulation and second was from the subscriptions.

The current circulation was 14,500 and their goal was to increase by 1,000 to 15,500. The per page advertising rate could be raised by $600 if they hit their goal. The $600 would go right to the bottom line as there was no additional cost except printing of the magazine, which would be covered by consumer purchase price. Each subscription is $55 annually, of which $28 is profit.

In order to provide incentive for the consumer to sign up for a two year subscription, the magazine offered an MP3 player speaker. The cost of the speaker and fulfillment was $18.50. After 5 months, the magazine reached its goal of 1000 additional subscribers. The investment was $18,500 for the speakers and mailers. And there was a $4250 increase in printing and mailing for the additional magazines. The return, however, was impressive. There was an additional $28,000 in profit from subscriptions (for one year. There was also an additional $79,200 additional profit from advertisers for the next 6 months. So the return on their investment was $84,450 or 370%!

More on Promotional Products!

Now you might be asking, "What about trade shows?" And you would be smart to do so! Promotional products can be an intricate part of a successful trade show and that is why I am dedicating an entire chapter to it!

For more creative ideas and case studies for utilizing promotional products into your marketing campaign, check out our website at: www.hassemanmarketing.com.

Big Marketing for Trade Shows

So you have a big trade show coming up and you want to make an impact. How do you make the BIG impact without breaking the marketing budget for the whole year? By creating a targeted marketing plan for the show of course!

So many companies, realizing they have a trade show on the horizon, decide to quickly get a cheap backdrop and some "giveaways" and believe they have done their job. They spend the money to display at the show and commit to the travel budget. They hand out flyers and pens and wonder why their return is not high. Why aren't the sales just rolling in? They spent money…but with no plan. What a waste!

Let's face it. If you have chosen this trade show correctly, then these are *very* targeted potential customers for you. So you should obviously spend the time and energy to convert them from potential clients…to customers!

Create Your Theme for the Show

This may sound a bit like work, but it really is not that hard. Just start with your theme. If your company has a theme that you have created for the year/quarter/season then that might fit the bill. If the show has a theme, then you might decide to tie into that. And, hey, if the two coincide…even better! But either way, create a simple theme that you plan to follow in *all* of your marketing efforts. Have some fun with this! The idea for the trade show is to reach new clients…so be creative and memorable!

Create Pre-show Buzz

This is where so many businesses cut back on their trade show budgets. I understand the need to keep expenses down whenever possible, but if you have allotted the money to be here, you might as well do it right. And if you can change the return rate from 5% to 25%, then your efforts will be totally worth it!

In order to create the pre-show buzz, get the list of all attendees to the show. Most shows will gladly provide this for you. This *targeted* list of businesses will not only be a great source for creating pre-show buzz but will also be a source for your next direct mail campaign (see next chapter). With this list it's time to create your pre-show mailer that will get them thinking that they need to come and see you! And if it doesn't do that, the least it should do is have them remember you when they do walk by!

Again, the name of the game here is to have fun. You want to be memorable with this mailer…and there are lots of ways to do that. Make sure it fits your (and your company's) personality and go for it!

I have seen company's send out a puzzle piece that can be turned into the booth to see if they win a prize. You could mail out a card and ask them to bring it to your booth to get a free t-shirt. Or you can simply mail out a colorful postcard to all participants. And obviously you can do better than this. As I said, make a splash!

Look and Feel of the Booth

Now that you have created your pre-show buzz, you want to make sure the look and feel of your booth is sharp. Of course you will not be creating a new booth for each show you attend, so it might not completely portray the theme you have for the show (unless it is the theme for the whole year!), but it still needs to have some consistency in look to the rest of the material.

In addition, the look and feel of the booth is not just about the backdrop! Make sure your staff is well represented in their attire and attitude! If you want them to be a representative of your company and your brand, make sure they have the apparel to do so. This might mean outfitting them all in the same logoed shirt and similar colored pants/skirts. Or it might be something really fun that fits the theme. I recently saw a booth that had a "beach theme." This company had designed their booth as a Tiki bar. They had surf boards and even sand on the floor. The staff was outfitted in Hawaian shirts, shorts and flip flops, and they were handing out non-alcoholic beers from the bar! Now that is riding the theme to the end! And guess what? There was a line into the Tiki to join the party!

Video at the Trade Show

When considering the look and feel of the booth, it is a great time to decide whether to integrate video as well. This depends on many factors (budget not being the least!) but should only be used if you think you can really do it right.

Video can be a nice substitute for those times when you and all of your staff are busy with other interested clients. Those who are willing to wait will be able to hear your story a bit until they have a moment to chat with you personally. Video at a trade show can often be your salesperson when you are not available.

You also might consider a video if your product has a visually interesting manufacturing process. Showing the potential client the way the product is put together is often a way to communicate the quality and integrity of the product and the company. In addition, some people are simply interested in how things go together…so you might grab someone's attention long enough for them to talk to you!

But if you are going to incorporate video into the booth, make sure you incorporate it into the look. Don't just throw a TV up after the fact…it will look like it. Make the video presentation look as professional as the rest of your space!

Who Is in Your Booth?

I just want to touch briefly on who you are going to have in your trade show booth. Though each company and sales person might have a different style, make sure the representatives of your company are comfortable being in that role. So many times people will throw anyone (spouses, friends, secretaries, etc.) in that role and it is usually awful. And if you do find yourself in the position of having an inexperienced person be your rep…train them! But at the end of the day, do your best to have your "brand" be well represented at these functions. It will SO pay off!

The Promotional Piece

So we have gone all this way and we are just now mentioning the hand out for the show. That is because it is only a piece of the properly planned trade show. But it is a BIG piece! When done right, the proper targeted marketing piece can actually drive real traffic to your booth…just to get it! And done even more right…it reminds people what the hell you do after the show too! Like I said…it's a big piece!

So once you decide what your theme for the show is, the promotional piece will often fall into place easily. But if not, you need to ask yourself a couple of questions.

1) Do I want to make a big impact at the show? In other words, are you going to go with an item that drives traffic to your booth and is flashy the day of the show?

2) Do I want to make a big impact after the show? Or are you focused on giving attendees an item that they will keep on their desk/person for a time after the show so they will call after the show buzz has worn off?

3) Do I want to do both? There are items that certainly do this…but often budget does begin to become a factor.

There is no "right" answer to these questions. But they usually do help to guide you into the direction of where you want to go. I tend to try to shoot for number three when working with clients (Duh) and you may want to as well. When in doubt about what item to consider I always tell my clients that "Humans are simple creatures. If it lights up or flashes it will get our attention!"

CASE STUDY

Northside Pharmacy is a chain of retail pharmacy locations in Ohio. They had been a client for some time when we met about a trade show that they would be attending for the first time. They told me they wanted to make a "big splash" at the show so they wanted a really cool promotional handout to drive traffic to the booth. After discussing some less expensive giveaways that they had seen done before, I recommended spending a bit more for bigger impact. They agreed to give that a try and we decided on a nice pen that lights up.

The results were extremely impressive. Not only did Northside have lines all day to their trade show booth to get the giveaway, but they were voted "best promotional item" in the marketing classes. All in all, they made the big splash at the new trade show and had the leads to prove it!

The Big Follow-Up Plan

So now that you have spent the time, the energy and money it takes to do a successful trade show…there's more work! So many businesses attend the shows and hope that the interested parties will come to them. Crazy! Of course some folks will be so enamored by your theme, presentation, and giveaway that they will not be able to stay away. But many customers will have a million thoughts (and other vendors) running through their head so you will need to remind them why you were the best.

So now take all of the business cards and contacts you made at the show and get on the phone. It does not have to be an over the top sales job here. Just a follow up call will do. It could go something like this:

"Mr. Smith. This is Kirby Hasseman with Hasseman Marketing and we met the other day at the XYZ Trade Show. Thanks for stopping by our booth! You may remember we handle (whatever) for companies like yours and I just wanted to see if you needed any additional information from us?"

The Final Mailer

So there you have a comprehensive Trade Show marketing plan for your next big event. But do you remember the list you got from the Trade Show to begin with for your original mailer? One final step might be do a follow up mailer from the show to give them one more chance to fall in love with your company!

How do you make that mailer effective? We'll find out in the next chapter!

Thinking Big on Direct Mail

Direct mail is an important part of many successful small business marketing plans. But I have also seen so many small businesses waste thousands of dollars by doing it inefficiently...or just plain wrong! And let's face it, as postage and shipping costs continue to go up and up, screwing up here can cost your business a lot!

Targeting the List

As you can imagine (since we have been harping on targeting your marketing so far) we believe in making sure whatever list you have is a targeted one. Even if you are working from a very large list, do your very best to make sure this is a list with people who might want or need your product or service.

So much advertising and marketing is wasted on those who have no interest whatsoever in the product in front of them. Hence the term "junk mail." Don't waste your money to create junk mail! If you work to make sure the group of people is pre-disposed to having a need for your company and its product or service, then your likelihood for some direct mail success increases exponentially!

Make the Letter Count

I must admit, I am not a fan of just sending a letter in an envelope. To me that is WAY too easy to dispose of. But I also understand that cost is often an issue and you will sometimes want to reach a great deal of folks with a small budget. So let's take a look at a couple of quick thoughts on your basic direct mail letter.

Colored Envelopes Get Attention: I know that white envelope is cheaper. But when you consider the cost of the letter based on the return, the extra couple of cents might be worth it if the percentage return increases. Think of ways to get the recipients attention…and colored envelopes might help!

Handwrite the Name and Address: This might be the oldest trick in the book…but it works. People are much more likely to open a hand addressed envelope. And of course if you can get them to open it, you are way ahead of those neatly printed ones that end up in the circular file. As a side note, if you don't have time to handwrite thousands of letters (I know I don't) then there are services out there that will address them for you.

Keep It Concise: There are several schools of thought on this, but I am always in favor of the Keep It Simple Stupid (K.I.S.S.) method. If it takes me a long time to wade through a message, it is more likely to be tossed. Catch my attention early and you might get me to stay around!

Use a Postcard: Reconsider whether you need an actual letter to tell the story. Often you can tell your story faster on a postcard and you get attention right away. The potential client is less likely to throw the message away before he/she sees it if she HAS to see it in order to throw it away! Full color has come way down on things like this so you can produce a nice, eye-catching piece for not too much money.

Consider Your Offer Carefully: Most direct mail offers something. At worst, it's information that perhaps your prospect didn't have; at best, it's something none of your prospects can afford to ignore. If your offer is a free car for responding, your response rate will go through the roof, but your cost will be too much. If you offer a packet of salt from a diner…it may not cause anyone to respond. Offer *something* beyond information to cause your recipient to take action! What that is depends on your audience and your business; it doesn't have to be much. Which segues nicely to…

Use BuMpY Mail!

If a letter is the only way to communicate your message, or if you want to include several things in the mailing, you will have to use an envelope. What I recommend in these cases is to use what I call BUMPY Mail! Put simply, this is when you get a letter in the mail that has "something" inside of it. It could be a pen, or a keychain, or a damn koala bear for all we know. But there is something in that envelope that makes in bumpy…and we HAVE to know what!

Of course there are going to be additional postage charges for something like this. But as we know, we need to judge the cost on response rate. If you want to get your letters opened...make the envelope bumpy!

Don't Forget Packaging

So let's combine the bumpy mail concept with the post card concept (or even the colored envelopes) and take it to the next level. We spend SO much time in business worrying about the grammar, spelling, the message, the font, the logos, and the offers on the inside of the package, that we often forget about the package! So I would encourage you, as a small business owner, to spend just as much time on the outside of the package. Done correctly, this will help get the attention of the recipient and lead them to the "secrets on the inside" of the envelope.

What do I mean? Well of course we have mentioned that you could use colored envelopes. Okay. And don't forget about making the package bumpy...got it. What else can you do to make it stand out? Can you print "Free OFFER inside" on the envelope to make it more interesting? Yep. What about telling people, "Don't Open Unless You LOVE Money?" Okay...you've got my attention. The fact is, spend more time thinking about what would move your trigger as a consumer on the *outside* of the package or box!

Find Your Watermelon!

One of my favorite examples of this comes from a trade show I attended years ago. I was at a class and it changed the way I viewed packaging in marketing. The presenter was talking about the importance of utilizing packaging. In doing so, he told us the story of a colleague that HAD to get a message to just 6 people. She could not take the chance of her recipients missing it in the mail or simply thinking it was "junk mail." What to do?

So the ingenious woman took a Sharpie and wrote the message on 6 watermelons! She played hell with the post office, but after a LOT of conversation, she got them mailed overnight to the 6 destinations. At this point the presenter stopped from pacing to look at the group and said, "So I ask you. You come to work Monday morning and there is a Watermelon sitting on your desk...do you read it?!" The class erupted in laughter and applause!

The moral of the story is: Stand Out if you want to be noticed in direct mail. Do something wild and out of the ordinary if you are looking to land that big fish. One of my favorite mailers that a sales person I know does is a large Rubber Duck. It's about 12 inches tall…and it's a real Rubber Ducky! He includes a funny letter and the response rate is phenomenal!

So find your Watermelon…and watch your response rate go through the roof on direct mail!

Follow Up Is Key!

As is the case with all business, follow up is so important. You can have the best direct mail campaign, but if there is no follow up, there will always be a ceiling to your success. If you can better target your market so that you can better follow up on your mailers, then you will find that direct mail can become an enormous part of your Think Big Marketing Success!

CASE STUDY

Several years ago, one of our salespeople called on a very modest business located at the time in the prospect's garage in a medium Midwestern city. Turns out the guy repaired speedometers (this was back when they were virtually all mechanical in construction and operation). He knew nothing about marketing, but he sure knew how to fix speedometers, and a few questions by the salesperson ascertained that virtually all auto repair shops, including dealers, sent out a broken speedometer for repair; no one had that expertise on staff. They were more concerned with fixing exhaust systems and engines.

The market was very specific: auto repair shops and dealership repair departments. The offer was easy: a money-back guarantee and the first one done at half-price. The job just cried out for direct mail as a primary marketing thrust.

The vehicle to mail featured a self-opening ("Pull here to open") window envelope with a black-and-white photo of what any grease monkey would recognize as a speedometer and the words "First One For Half Price!" The single-side printed card stock inside had more specific information, including

"Ship To" instructions and a guarantee of 48-hour turnaround…and the client—who knew his market—insisted on a hole drilled at the top of each card. He knew the recipient would hang the card on a nail or pin on opening it…where he could find it when the next broken speedometer came in his shop.

From an initial citywide mailing that cost $1,200, including printing and postage, the client's business grew by leaps and bounds, to regional success, then multiple states, then national…all based on this same card stock mailing. Eventually he began what he called "penetration marketing" by sending auto repair shops an imprinted calendar…once they'd sent him at least one speedometer order.

This program won a Bronze Echo Award from the Direct Marketing Association…and the Gold that year went to National Geographic Magazine; the Silver went to Ford Motor Company, who'd spent *$12 million* on their campaign. Not bad for a speedometer repair shop who started from a garage!

Big Marketing on the Web

First things first, I want to be clear that I am NOT a web designer or programmer. I am not interested in being one, and don't claim to have their expertise. I do, however, have a grasp of some (not all) of the things you can do to market your business online. I will relay a few of them here.

First business fact: It is a huge, ever expanding, exciting world online and you absolutely need to be a part of it.

And here's the other secret…it's really not has hard or expensive as many people believe. It just depends on what you want to create! So let's start with what kind of website you want.

Brochures vs. Business Machines

In my opinion there are two basic kinds of websites: Brochures and Business Machines. Which type of site you want for your business really depends on you want to accomplish with the site. For some businesses, a simple website that basically tells your products and services, contact information, and pictures can be fine. In essence this is your **brochure** online. Though you can certainly do more online, this is a good way to at least create a presence online. The Brochure website is fine for many businesses, as long as they keep some simple things in mind!

Keep the Brand Consistent: Make sure your brochure online matches the brochure you hand out to customers. I know this seems basic, but you would be surprised how many times the two are worlds apart. You don't want your potential customers to come to your site and think they are lost! I have seen it happen!

Capture Information: If you have a simple site that informs a potential customer about your services, and how to contact you, that is great. But make sure you have a mechanism in place to capture their information. This is the key! Many marketers believe that the goal in advertising it todays world is *not* to create a sale. Did you read that right? Yes…the goal of many advertising campaigns is to drive traffic to their website! Why? They do this because the power of getting potential customers to their website is so great. At the website, these marketers can NOT ONLY make the sale, but can up-sell them on other products, give them more information on their interest AND they can capture their email information. By doing this simple act, they are not gaining a customer…they are capturing a customer for life!

Keep It Functional: There are some pretty amazing graphics that can be done on a website these days. I say skip it (unless you are a graphics company!). Your goal should be to create a website that is easy to function for customers and quick to load. If your site has mind blowing graphics but is slow to load or difficult navigate you will lose them.

I once had a client tell me that my website was "boring." He wanted to show me a site that he thought was really cool. First, he couldn't remember the website's address (strike one) so he had to call someone to get it. When he tracked it down and showed me, it was impressive. But as he drug his mouse around the site he said, "I don't know how to get around here." At that point I stopped him. "If you can't remember the address and you can't navigate the site, it's not a good site." He didn't care for my analysis, but to this day I couldn't tell you what that site was trying to sell me!

Business Machines: The other type of website is what I call the Business Machine. This is the type of website that can be your online store. Though there are varying sizes and shapes of this brand of site, let's just say it's the kind of site you actually sell things from. This type of site can do all of the things that your Brochure site can do, but it can actually make you money too! It's your online shopping mall for the brand of YOU!

Obviously it depends on the type of business you are in whether this is the right kind of site for you. But don't be scared by how "hard" it is to set something like this up. So many would be online marketers are intimidated by this concept and they are giving up huge opportunities. With the eBay, Amazon, and all of the travel sites that are prevalent, customers are very accustomed to doing business online...and are getting more so!

In addition, it is getting easier to accept credit cards online as well. As you know, there are hundreds (if not thousands) of companies that will help you accept credit cards online. But if you just want to get your feet wet, it's really easy to set up a PayPal account too. PayPal is form of payment created at eBay that accepts all kinds of credit cards. They have done the work for you on this...it's really easy!

This almost goes without saying, but not quite. But if you want customers to place orders on your site, it needs to be easy. The percentage of overall purchases goes up substantially if your site is easy to navigate. So keep that in mind as you set it up. Make it easy for the customer to give you money!

Basically you need to understand that this is not as difficult as we sometimes believe. And I want you to understand that you need to have your business online (if it is not already). As someone told me recently, "They are going to have to do this in the next 2 years...so why not do it now?" So take a lesson from our friends at Nike...and Just Do It!

Marketing with eNewsletters: This topic is robust enough for an entire chapter, but for now let's just say you need to utilize this marketing weapon for your arsenal to be complete. Once you get customers to give you their email information, make sure you use this powerful and low cost marketing option by informing customers about special offers you have coming up. You know your customer base best, but I recommend creating a consistent e-marketing plan...and following it.

Some of my clients simply send out "specials" they are running at any given time. This can be a great way to drive sales. Other clients (and I would be included in this sector) create an eNewsletter and regularly send that out to clients. This way we are providing clients with real nuggets of knowledge, while promoting the products and services we offer. This way is a little more work, but I find it to be effective.

Make It Change: Once you have the website up and running, I believe you should make it change on a regular basis. What do I mean? The basic message and look of the site can stay the same, but give customers a reason to come back. You can have a special offer on the home page each week, you can have a special update on products, or you can constantly add features to the site. Just give your customers a reason to come back! Think of the sites you visit each day…they are different each day! Keep that in mind as you decide how often to change your site.

Commit to It: Once you have a website up and running and you are happy with its look and functionality, then you have to commit to it. As I mentioned earlier, many companies are using their advertising dollars just to drive traffic to their site. You need to do everything to you can to promote this new advertising tool. You should have the website on your advertising pieces, in your email signature, and on everything you have printed. Make sure you don't create this tool…and ignore it! Do everything you can do promote potential customers to your site!

E-Marketing…Targeted Keys to Big Success

One of the fastest growing tools in the smart small business person's marketing tool box is email. And when used properly, e-marketing can be one of the most powerful tools as well! With the correct "targeted" list, e-marketing combines the best that direct mail has to offer…with low or no cost! Now that is the right price!

But the key is to make sure you do your e-marketing right. And though there are many authors that spend entire books on just this subject…that is not what this book is about. So we are going to give you some quick tips to help you make sure your next e-marketing campaign is a huge success!

Get the List

If you are like me, you probably get both SPAM (the unwanted and annoying email marketing) and valuable, permission-based email marketing that you regularly open and read. Obviously you want your email marketing to be the latter! Not only is spam annoying, but there are regulations against spammers that you don't want to get involved in. So the first step in a good email marketing campaign is to get the right email list.

There are two obvious ways to "get the list." You can build your own permission based list or you can purchase one. There are advantages to both ways.

The downside to building your list yourself is that it can definitely be the "long way." You will need to contact your current clients to get their buy-in. In addition, you can have a tab on your website that encourages clients and prospects to sign up for your special deals or newsletter. Often, you can encourage a higher percentage to participate by offering a "special gift" or even special deals. Depending on your current website traffic, you can build this list relatively fast. But if you are just establishing your web presence this can take some time. On the other hand, I think this is the best way to establish a truly targeted and credible list!

The other way to get the list is to purchase it. As you can imagine, this is the faster way to get your e-marketing campaign started. The challenge you face with this prospect is making sure you get a list that is targeted to your product or service. It can be a huge list, with active emails, but worthless if they are not truly potential customers for you! Remember, we are all about TARGETED solutions here!

Sometimes the best way to "get the list" is a combination of these two strategies. You create whatever list of contacts you can with your current clientele, and then purchase a good list to drive traffic to your site. Then offer a limited time deal in order to promote the list on the site! There you have the best of both worlds to create a full and productive e-marketing target list!

Finally, make sure if you are selling products online that you capture that email address in the process. As we have mentioned in the past, you are advertising in order to create a customer for life...not just one sale!

Keep It Simple...and Brief!

Just like so many other effective marketing tools, you want your e-marketing campaign to be dynamic and brief. I recommend you try to get your initial offer in the very first glance of the email. Don't make the potential customer have to scroll far to get the information. If you need to add additional information (or better yet additional offers) then you can do that...but make sure they can see what you are offering right away.

In addition, if you have images that you are using to "sell" the product or service, then I recommend you embed them in the email. Though there are times you need to attach them to the email to be opened, I like it when my clients see an offer right away. I find that you lose a percentage each time you make them do an extra step. If you ask your potential customers to click on a link or open an attachment, some of them simply won't take the time unless they are already interested. How do you get them interested? Show them the offer, image or something unusual or interesting right as they open the email!

Drive Traffic to Your Site

Remember as you create your e-marketing campaign that the goal is to drive traffic to your website. As we have mentioned before, if you drive potential clients to your site, then you have the opportunity to gain a customer for life! And if you have crafted your email correctly, you can let them decide if they want to learn more about you or your company. So make sure you give them an opportunity to click on the link to your website. As a matter of fact, I have seen e-marketers utilize the strategy of giving potential customers MULTIPLE chances to click on links in the same email. It's a great way of increasing the percentage of click-thrus to your site!

Use Some Consistency in Delivery

I am a fan of developing a consistent e-marketing program. For example, my clients receive my marketing e-newsletter each Monday. Though there are some folks who will tell you this is too much (and some who will tell you it's not enough!) this is the right mix for me. My clients know that each Monday they will get a message from me…so there are no surprises. Often, they come to look for the message because I am not blasting offers and emails at them every day. But on the other side, if I only sent them every once in a while, they would not know what it was and might delete it. Each client base will be different, so I would leave your frequency up to you. But I encourage you to make it consistent.

Add Value to the Clients

There are a couple of ways to add value to the client through your e-marketing efforts. The first way is a product driven way. Through your consistent e-marketing message, you can consistently offer fantastic deals that your customers look for…and value! "Where is that special this week?" Another way to add value is to create an informational newsletter with valuable tidbits of information in it. They can look for your newsletter to provide inspiration each week…and that adds value!

In my e-newsletter I try to do a little of both. Each week I focus on a marketing theme for my clients...and I focus on a product or service as well. It's a little more work, but it can be extremely effective!

Get to the Point!

As we have discussed throughout this book, I am a fan of brevity when it comes to marketing messages. Though there are exceptions, most long and involved marketing messages simply get missed. People are too busy to spend time reading every long email they get! (I understand that there are folks that have had success with more robust email campaigns. But these are exceptions with great writers involved. Most of us are not scriptwriters...so get to the point!). So just like the case of this book...get to the point in your e-marketing campaign and let customers come to you to get more information!

I will end this chapter with a Top Ten List of sorts. Here are 10 tips for email marketers!

1. Only send emails to persons who have requested it. Don't SPAM. It's unwanted, ineffective and will tarnish your company's reputation.
2. Only include content relevant to the person who requested it.
3. Be consistent with your sending frequency. Pick a schedule and stick to it.
4. In most cases, send B2B emails Tuesday through Thursday. Send them around 9:30 or 1:30. It's best to avoid B2B emails after 4pm or on weekends.
5. Business to consumer emails should go 5pm to 8pm Tuesday-Thursday or Friday evening to Sunday afternoon.
6. To improve deliverability add a message at the top of your emails that says something like: To ensure receipt of our emails, please add kirby@hassemanmarketing.com to your Address Book.
7. Make the from name of the email either the company name or the name of the person sending it. Once you choose that name, keep it. During the split second decision subscribers make whether to open your email, the most important facor in their decision is whether they recognize the FROM name.

8. When possible in clued both a plain text and HTML message. 5% of those receiving the message will only see a message with nothing if you don't do this. Most email management companies help you do this.

9. Don't use all caps or multiple exclamation points within your subject line or body. Doing this will trigger spam filters.

10. Build your list at every opportunity. If you have retail locations, add a point of sale sign up form. At conferences or events ask everyone you speak with if you may add them to your list after you exchange cards. Finally, add your newsletter sign up form to every page on your website.

At the end of the day, email marketing is a tool in the marketing tool box...but it's a good one. I don't recommend my clients have any one tool...but to use utilize a variety of tools that work best for you. But if your organization is not using email marketing, then you are certainly missing opportunities!

This Chapter's To-Do List:
1. Get the List
2. Craft your message
3. Drive traffic to your site
4. Create consistent delivery
5. Add Value to Customer
6. Keep it brief

Big Appreciation Marketing

Making Thank You Work for You!

The most under used words in business are "thank you." Let's face it…as a business owner; you get busy with the bills, the orders, the follow up, the promotion, the invoicing, the staff and more! It's difficult to stop and take the time to truly say "thank you" to the clients who make all of that work worthwhile! It's tough to find the time!

That being said, it is one of the most valuable strategies a business owner can implement to help maintain, and yes grow, your business!

Happy Customers = More Business

There are a million books and sources out there that tell you it is easier to do business with a current customer than to go out and get a new one. It's not new information. But it's also important to note that it is easier to do *more* business with a current customer than to find a new one too! Happy Customers already trust you. Happy Customers already see a value in what you have to offer.

So don't take those Happy Customers for granted. First of all, make sure you are regularly marketing directly to those current customers. Whether you have their information from your website (check that chapter) or from purchases they have made in your place of business, make sure you are selling (and upselling) to that current base.

In addition, make sure you are thanking those customers! By thanking those customers regularly you are reminding them how much they like doing business with you. And when your customers like doing business with you, they become a fantastic source of referrals. These referrals make your business of marketing and prospecting a much easier task…because your customers are doing it for you!

Just think…by simply providing the best service and product you can…and then thanking those who utilize…you can create a constant source of business growth! Thank You really can be a powerful marketing tool!

So let's assume you buy in to the Thank You Program. You have made it a part of your business culture. You have instructed all of your staff to end each transaction with a sincere "thank you" to the customer. You have created a new coupon program just for your current customer base. And you now have a mailing list that you send (or email) special offers to regularly in order to add value to your business relationship. These are all fantastic ways to create a "thank you" culture in your business. But here are some other ways to regularly and tangibly thank your customers!

Quarterly Thank You Program

One way to consistently show your customers a level of appreciation is to create a Quarterly Thank You Program. It's easy, and can be a low cost way to reach out to your best clients. Most companies have a client base with the 80/20 rule. 80% of the revenue comes from 20% of the clients or customers. This may not always be true, but it is amazing how often it is. (So for the sake of this discussion let's assume this is true. But if your company's percentages are different, simply fill them in and use the idea).

Find the 20% of your client base that brings in 80% of your sales. Got that number? Now decide on a basic dollar amount that you will be willing to spend to personally "thank" that customer. Remember…these are your best clients. Would you be willing to spend $10 to thank each of them for their business loyalty? Once you have that number budgeted, select a gift in that range and send it to them (or personally drop it off) with a personal note thanking them for their business! You can choose anything to be in that range, but I recommend a nice promotional item with your contact information on it! This gives this simple gesture some long lasting marketing value.

Now do this each quarter in order to consistently give those top customers a "promotional hug!" I recommend meeting with your promotional consultant to place these orders regularly. If your consultant is a good one, they should let you place all 4 quarters orders at once and then have them shipped at the desired time. If you do this, then it will help you ensure the program consistency. When the next shipment arrives, you know it's time to send them out! By implementing this one program, you can regularly thank your best customers consistently!

Year End Gift Program

If you are not ready to implement the Quarterly Thank You Program (or you just want to add to it) then a simple Year End Gift Plan can be a nice touch. Again, the simple act of thanking a customer for their business loyalty can be a truly powerful thing. But one thing I always recommend is to give something here that can give you lasting value for your marketing dollar.

So many businesses utilize food during the holidays, and that can be a very appreciated gift for an entire office, but I always caution that you should find a way to add a long term marketing message to it! How? First of all, there are lots of cool ways to emblazon your company logo on chocolate, and other food items. But you could also simply do more than one gift. Bring the food for the office, but a nice personalized wall calendar for your best contacts there. Again, work with your promotional consultant to get ideas that fit your budget.

Direct Contact with Clients

If you decide to implement either of these ideas, don't be afraid to go out and see your clients to deliver the "thank you" message. Sometimes this is not feasible, but it can be a very powerful way to drive home how much you appreciate their business! Though you are simply going to a client to say "thanks" you will be very surprised by how often they suddenly need something you have to sell...right then!

Customer Appreciation Event

If you are looking for a way to make your customers extra special and really separate yourself from the competition, then a Customer Appreciation Event is a great way to go! Though it can be a more costly endeavor, it can really be powerful "thank you" and even a great selling tool. And there are some ways to be creative and make this event happen without breaking the bank. I have included these tips in a special chapter dedicated just to the Customer Appreciation Event.

But trust me, if you can implement these "Thank You Marketing" tools, you can really help to solidify your current client base...and position yourself for future growth!

To-Do List:
1. Create a Thank You Culture in your business.
2. Begin a Quarterly Thank You Program.
3. Take it up a notch during the Holidays.
4. Go and See the People to thank them directly!
5. Host a Customer Appreciation Event!

Big Event Marketing

Making a Big Impact with a Small Budget!

Do you want to have a marketing ploy that not only gives you an opportunity to say "thank you" to your customers, but also represents an opportunity to truly separate yourself from your competition? Then you might consider creating a customer appreciation event for your company!

Done right, a customer appreciation event can give you the opportunity to spend time with your clients away from the office…and help to sell services you might not have had the chance to sell before. In addition, it helps to solidify those business relationships you have worked so hard to cultivate.

Big Event…Small Budget

"Sure!" You might be thinking, "I would love to cradle my clients in adoration, but I don't have the budget to do it right!" As ESPN analyst Lee Corso might say, "Not so fast, my friend!" You can create a great event for not a huge amount of money with some creative thinking. You don't necessarily need a party planner for this great company event!

In addition, just consider what you are considering to spend your money on. It very likely can be an extremely valuable opportunity to get in front of your best customers in a new way…or an extended period of time. It can allow you to up-sell new services or products. And of course it can be a great opportunity to just say "thank you" in a dynamic and impressive fashion. It might be worth the dollars!

So how do you spend small? This is where you need to be creative! Look for chances to barter here. Can you provide services or products for a local caterer in order to get the food for free or deeply discounted? Do you need to rent a facility or can you save money (and maybe have a better opportunity to up sell) in your own location? Can you get suppliers or business partners to help you with demos or displays or even giveaways? As you look at the entire event plan, look at every chance to save money. You want it to be a cool event…but you don't want it to break the bank!

Making It a Big Event

There are many options to add for attracting clients and making it a special event. Although each company is going to want to focus on different things, there are some basics that can help to make it big!

Food and Drinks: If you are going to have a Customer Appreciation Event then you better have something to eat and drink. Free food is the perfect reason for someone to visit your event if they are considering. I also like to have it over lunch or just after work to make sure they are hungry! This can be an expensive part of the event, so you need to consider what you want to spend here. My company does a Customer Appreciation Event each year and we keep it pretty simple. It doesn't have to be a 7 course meal, but something to eat is smart. You know your clientele…so just make sure it is appropriate.

Make It Exclusive: Sometimes it is appropriate to open your event up to the whole world, but I love the idea of making a Customer Appreciation Event an "invitation only" affair. It really adds value to the event and makes your customers feel special. When you ask them to present their invitations at the door, it brings home the fact that they are a part of something special. And as a side bonus, this is a huge help in keeping your costs down on the event as well!

Have a Theme: Though this is not a necessity, it's an easy thing to help you guide the event. Your theme can help you consider decorations (if you want them) and invitations (yes you should have these). In addition, don't be afraid to dress the part too! The whole idea of the event (especially if it is in your place of business) is that this is NOT every day. Wear a tux or an evening gown! Again…you know your clients, but you can really make the event feel different by your clothes…and it doesn't cost much more!

Along the lines of a theme, don't be afraid to have music to enforce the mood. This is just a small touch that can help. Remember to consider all of the senses of the guest at the event. This does NOT have to cost a lot…just show them you have gone to the trouble of considering it!

Add a Speaker: This may or may not be appropriate…but it can really add credibility to the event. I am not suggesting you hire Tony Robbins to come and talk to your clients (I am probably available!) but a speaker can add value to the clients. Don't want to pay for it? Okay…think of your suppliers, organizations you are a part of, etc. There might be someone in those affiliations that would do it for free. As I said it may or may not be appropriate…just something to consider!

Give Them Something to Remember It By: After you have created this magical event that your customers loved, make sure they leave with something in their hands. With my event, we give them something as they come through the door (usually a tote bag and something to write with) and then I give them a nicer gift as the leave. I want them to remember the event with a warm and fuzzy feeling…and these gifts help! In addition, they provide a longer lasting promotional piece that clients can utilize for a long time!

So those are a few tips on making your Customer Appreciation Event a Big Marketing tool. And what a great targeted marketing piece as well! If you are considering taking this step (and it can be a big one) make sure you go full speed on promoting it! A great event will not do you any good if you don't get anyone to attend! So email them, mail them an invitation, and personally remind them! It can be a great marketing tool…just make sure they are there to enjoy it!

As I mentioned above, we at Hasseman Marketing began doing a Customer Appreciation event a few years ago with great success. We rent a local hall in order to have enough space and have one of our clients do the catering. They are a great friend so they discount the food quite a bit to help us keep this portion of the cost down. We have historically borrowed the local Rotary club's sound system (my wife is a member of that club) and we invite promotional suppliers to setup and show their lines to my customers. It's been a huge win-win-win scenario. We get to sincerely thank the customers for their continued support of our business. Our suppliers get one on one time with customers. And my customers get all the time they need to truly "shop" through promotional ideas that they have not seen. And the with the collaboration we have with our business partners, our cost has been kept to a relative minimum…with a BIG bottom line impact!

Marketing Through Networking Groups and Giving Back

Many business owners understand the inherent value in being a part of networking groups. The opportunity to get together and rub shoulders with business owners in your geographic area (or area of expertise) can be fertile ground to prospect! And most networking groups do a great job of promoting their own members to each other. Whether it's your local Chamber of Commerce or another business networking group, this can be an easy way to promote your business.

But I want to take this a step further. As you consider groups to join in order to promote your business, I want to encourage you to join groups that "give back" to the community as well. Organizations like Rotary, Kiwanis, Lions can not only be a source of great networking and business opportunities, but they make a difference.

So why does that matter? Lots of reasons, folks.

Let's start from a business perspective. When you work together on projects in an organization like this, you form strong bonds with fellow service club members. There is something truly powerful about spending a Saturday afternoon helping others to build a new shelter in the community. You laugh together. You cuss together. You sweat together. And at the end of the day, you have built something together. And when they decide to purchase the service or product that you offer, they will remember that Saturday afternoon. They will remember that time you spent together.

Let's face it…people still buy from people (when possible). And you will be the person that person goes to first! These organizations are good for business. And though a simple networking group is good for business too, there is little doubt that those relationships are not as strong as the one you created that Saturday afternoon.

Now let's discuss the intrinsic value of the service organization. There are many folks who believe that the universe is tilted in favor of those who do well by others. One of my favorite books, "The One Minute Millionaire" is based on that concept. They argue that if you spend the first 10% of what you earn on charitable giving, blessings will return to you ten-fold. I love that. So any organization that allows me to promote my business while being able to do good in my own community is a great win-win!

But if you do join one of these organizations, make sure you make the most of it. So many business owners join their local Rotary Club only to go to lunch every Tuesday. Though you can certainly gain some contacts by going about it this way, these organizations are much like life. You get out of them only what you put in. Make sure you pitch in on weekend projects, attend board meetings, and go the extra mile. Apart from the input you will have on your organization, each of these will be an opportunity to become a person of influence in your community!

And to build upon this idea of supporting your community, let me take this opportunity to encourage you to give back. This is not some political statement. I have found that some of the most powerful marketing decisions I have made have been to support local charities. These organizations and people remember who support them. Though I do caution that you shouldn't do this based on the "advertising benefits" you will receive. You will be disappointed. My suggestion is only that, in my experience, those who are most generous in their success are often rewarded in business as well as the heart.

So make sure you make the most of any networking group in your area, by joining and taking part. You never know when the next contact you make might be your next big fish!

Targeted Marketing with Radio

Some people might think that when I talk about "thinking big" and being "targeted" I might be discussing two distinctly different topics. But a really good radio marketing campaign can certainly be both "big" and "targeted" at the same time.

Targeting with Radio...Get the Facts!

Although each market is different, most areas you will be targeting will likely have multiple radio stations. And of course there are all kinds of stations to choose from. There are country stations, pop stations, rap, talk, and every genre in between. When choosing your targeted radio station, knowing your ideal target customer will be paramount.

If you have a basic idea of your customer, then make the radio station sales person show you the numbers. Most radio stations have some numbers on the demographics of their listenership. How many people are listening? What do they look like? What do they make? Press your sales person for this information and make sure it jives with the customers you are trying to attract.

Music or Talk Radio

As you know, there are many different types of radio stations (and even more with the onset of satellite radio) and that gives your company lots of options for advertising on radio. It's important to remember your targeted audience when choosing...but there are some basic concepts to remember. Music radio can be a more of a background sound in the car or office, so sometimes ads can drop into the background as well. Talk radio (politics, sports, religion stations, etc) are more of an active listening experience. The advantage of an active listening experience is that the ads might be more likely to be heard initially. On the other side, talk radio is less likely to be on in the office or during conversation…so the choice will be up to you!

Results Based Experiment

Still not sure what stations will be best for your company or product? The fact is, you might be trying to cross demographic lines and reach new audiences. So try this:

Create 5 different ads for your company with 5 distinctly different offers. Run each ad on a different radio station and genuinely track the results. (This will absolutely NOT work if you don't track the results). When you see which stations are getting you the most return, move your radio marketing dollars to those stations and scrap the others.

Get Your Message Across

Once you have decided to utilize radio, it's time to make sure you get the message right! If you have a brand, theme, or basic company message, you want to make sure you keep your ads consistent. It's great to have a distinctive sound that says "Your Company" before the first words come out. If you have a distinctive voice (even if it's not necessarily a great radio voice) you might be able to use that to your advantage. It's important to get the listener's attention…and you want to use any tool you have to do it (without being an obnoxious turn-off).

Once you have the basic company message (and you should have some idea of this based on earlier chapters!), don't be afraid to bang the drum. What do I mean? I mean you have paid for the spot, so make sure the listener **doesn't** leave wanting more! You need to give them an opportunity to hear where to contact you or find you. I tell my clients to mention their name or product at least 3 times in the ad if possible. In addition, mention the contact information repeatedly as well. I have heard extremely effective ads that do nothing but repeat their contact information over and over. The whole idea is to drive traffic to you…so give the listener every opportunity to find you!

Have a Unique Sound

This might seem redundant, but your ads should have your own sound. I am blown away by business owners who tell radio sales people to "just write it up and show it to me." How can they possibly know your business better than you? If you are not a good writer...that's fine. But at least give them some very seriously considered talking points to write from. Or...hire someone to write the ad for you.

This is the face you are going to present to potential customers. It needs to break through the other ads on the air to grab attention AND it needs to convey your message. It's a big job. And the owner of the business damn sure should have some input!

Music or No Music: This is really a judgment call for the advertiser. I am a believer in music when appropriate. It can help the ad seem more professional and can fill in dead spots (not that there should be any). In addition, the right music can help to set the tone for the ad and get attention. But keep in mind, the opposite can be true as well! Choose the wrong tone and it can kill a good ad! Again, be picky here. It's your face to the public and you should not apologize for wanting it to be just right!

Two Other Thoughts on the Sound of the Ad: When it's appropriate, don't be afraid to use two different voices on the ad. It's a quick trick to get the listener's attention and it can work. Also...some radio stations will allow you to ad a "tag" on the ad at the end. This allows you to promote some limited time special with the DJ doing it live. This can be an extremely effective way to grab attention and promote a special you have at the moment!

Drive Traffic to Your Best Front

This goes back to the concept of advertising driving traffic where you and your company can best "sell" yourself. Maybe you need to get actual foot traffic through the store...then spend time getting them to your location. If you do a lot (or would like to do a lot) of phone business, then the phone number mentioned repeatedly. And of course if you have a viable website, then you can certainly spend time driving them to that site. *Keep in mind though, that if your customers are listening in the car then they might have a tough time writing long numbers or websites down.*

Commit to the Campaign

This is where "committing to the message" comes into play. You have heard me say this before, but marketing of any kind will only work if the advertiser is willing to commit to it. You simply can't run one ad and expect droves of customers to rush to your doors (real or virtual). If you are going to run a radio campaign, then you really need to give it the exposure and time it deserves to be successful! If you are not going to commit to the idea, then save your money! This does not mean you should stick with something that is not working or you are getting poor feedback. It simply means you need to give the message time to break through!

Keys to Radio Marketing:

1. Get the Facts of the Radio Demographics
2. Choose the stations to advertise on
3. Create your Radio Message
4. Drive the Message Home
5. Experiment for station results
6. Drive them to your best "front"

Big Marketing with Contact Calls

Hand to Hand Contact for Your Company

One of the most inexpensive and yet effective ways to market your small business (especially in the early days) is to go out and "see the people." And ironically, it's one of the last things most small business owners want to do! I understand. Even the most seasoned salespeople would like to avoid the prospect of "cold calling." That's why I have come up with a less intimidating system for the process of going out and "seeing the people." *(Below we outline a very basic sales strategy. There are thousands of sales books on the market. If you want more detailed information on sales, we can recommend some we like at the end of the book!).*

The Tough Call
Don't let me fool you. Even as a person who began his business career in sales, the initial prospect of cold calling every day wore me out. That's why you want to create a nice customer list...so you don't have to do it!

Why is it so tough? It's tough because there is a chance of up close and personal rejection! It's hard not to take it personal. But that personal aspect is also what makes it so effective! It's very easy to be rude to a sales person on the phone. It's a piece of cake to delete an email without a second thought. It's a bit tougher to be a jerk in person (not impossible mind you!). So you will often get more of a chance to "sell yourself" in person.

Contact Calling
But just because it's tough does not mean you shouldn't do it. For some of us, the success of our business can depend on it! So we have created a simple,

easy, and effective way to get in front of potential customers. It's called the Contact Call.

I call it the Contact Call because that is all you want to be able to accomplish…to make contact. In a nutshell, you want to get into a business or organization that you identify. You want to identify the person who is most likely to purchase your product or service…and get his or her contact information. If possible, it would be great to talk to that person (not a necessity). And then you want to move on. It's that simple.

What? I didn't say anything about selling in there, did I? No…in this case you are trying to identify customers and get their contact information for future sales. You also want to establish some credibility initially (and most of the time that does NOT come from a quick and forced sale). And you want to get permission to call back and talk to them again. Then you will have the opportunity to make your sales pitch when they are in a more open and buying attitude! Let's get into more details.

How We Do It

Let's look at the way this might work through the eyes of a business owner doing Contact Calling!

Amy is the owner of a new business handling phone systems for larger companies. She is looking to grow her business quickly before doing any large scale marketing. Since she has done her Thing Big Marketing Plan, she has identified her business's strengths and who her most likely customer might be.

So we start with her heading out to a large industrial park close to her office. She understands (through very minimal research) that most businesses in this park have more than 50 to 100 employees and could benefit from the phone systems her company has to offer. She has 15 business cards with her and has determined that she will not go home until she has given them all out to potential customers. She is ready.

Amy breathes through the butterflies in her stomach. She grabs her folder (with brochures and cards in it) and walks through the double doors into the lobby of XYZ Company. She is greeted, as she walks through the door, by a woman behind a desk in the atrium. This person is obviously an administrative person…or a gatekeeper. It is often this person's job to shoo away unwanted sales people. (And as a business owner, you may know that there is often value in doing so!).

But Amy smiles confidently and says: "Hi. My name is Amy Proper from Proper Phone Services. I was wondering if you might be able to tell me the name of the person who handles your phone services here at XYZ."

Though Amy might not have had luck if she had asked to see this person right way, the gatekeeper can usually give you their name easily. After writing their name down in her notebook, Amy proceeds on.

"Great…thanks! I know it might be a long shot, but are they in today? I wanted to see if I could quickly introduce myself…and maybe set up an appointment for another time."

Now this will either work…or not. If it does not get you to see them…then Amy would follow up with: "I totally understand! Is there any chance that I might get their business card so I can set up an appointment for another time?"

Most of the time, this is a no-brainer. The gatekeeper knows that if they give you this information, then you will be gone. Once I get this, I usually like to leave a card and a brochure on the off chance they look at it. But that is just me!

Now if it does work—and you get to see your contact—keep it short! You want to immediately show them you value their time and are not trying to just con them into a quick sale. So in this situation, Amy would say:

"Thanks so much for taking a second Mr. Smith. I know you are busy! My name is Amy Proper and I own Proper Phone Services. I just wanted to take a second to introduce myself and personally give you my company's brochure and my card. Since I know you are busy I wanted to see if I could get your card…and call back to set up an appointment when you have time!"

This is an easy one for most folks. Most people will simply say "Sure. Give me a call and we can set something up." And sometimes you have someone who will want to see you now. That's great! But if you have gotten this far, then this call is a home run!

Now Amy has the Contact, The Card, and she even has permission to call back and set up an appointment. She has succeeded in her first Contact Call of the day! Now she heads down the road for her next…and when the day is done she will have a pocket full of prospects for her to follow up with!

Follow Up Is the Key

This almost goes without saying…but not quite. Obviously Contact Calling will get you nowhere if you don't properly follow up. So once you have successfully spent a day Contact Calling, make sure you take the time to follow up by setting up appointments. If you don't, you have wasted a lot of your own time. That call might go like this:

"Mr. Smith, this is Amy Proper from Proper Phone Services. I wanted to give you a call to follow up on our brief conversation from Monday. Do you have any time next week when we could get together and chat in more detail? I think Proper Phone Services could really be a benefit to your company."

Not everyone will say "yes" in this scenario, but in my experience the percentages will go up. And as you know, in marketing (and in sales) it is a numbers game. Do your best to make the numbers work in your favor!

So pick up the phone and call to make those appointments to close the sale. If you can consistently follow this strategy, you will soon find you have enough clients to move on to Appreciative Marketing…but that is for another chapter!

Now get out there and make Contact!

Big Marketing with Your Business and Staff

Everything Matters!

Many small business owners feel like they do their marketing when they are advertising. They believe if they spend enough dollars on their marketing efforts, then their marketing is complete. They would be wrong.

Everything Matters

As a small business owner, you need to understand that every piece of the business speaks to the marketing of the company. What do I mean? I mean simply that you can have the best advertising in the world...but if your place of business is dirty and unattractive, you will not reach your sales goals. Each piece of your business has a big effect (notice I didn't just say an effect) on your marketing efforts.

So as a business owner you need to consider all things a part of your marketing. What does your business location look like? Is it clean and inviting? Is it bright? I am not just talking about your signage here. Of course that is a part of your marketing! But you need to understand that the look of your business is often the only "first impression" your business gets! Make sure it's the one you want!

Don't have a physical location? What about your demeanor (or your employees' demeanor) on the phone? Does your company have a positive phone presence? Does the phone at your establishment get answered with a smile and friendly helpful tone? Yep...that's marketing too!

What about the colors your staff wears? Have you considered that to be a part of your marketing? It is. I am not suggesting you have to have uniforms (though that is often a nice option), but you need to consider what your customers see when they are dealing with your company. There are many studies that say a good, professional look (and even specific colors) can make a buying difference.

The point is, everything matters when it comes to marketing your business. Make sure you do sweat some of the little details because they will matter to your customers. And if it matters to your customers—and your sales—then it is marketing!

Marketing During the Sale

When you or your staff is talking to your customer during the sales process you can have a big impact on your marketing as well. (As you can see, I believe your marketing and your overall business success are closely tied together!).

I am a big believer in an inquisitive sales method. If you or your staff take the time to ask questions of clients or customers, you not only show your customers that you are truly concerned with their needs, but you also get a better idea on how to meet them. And from a purely profit-oriented focus, you have a better idea on what they might need in addition to what they are currently buying. Up-selling is a great bottom line booster!

So when you are working with a client, take the time to truly listen to the customer. It might sound cliché', but it works! There is nothing more frustrating than seeing a loyal customer with a competitor's product and hearing "I didn't know you did that!" You know when you hear that, that you did not take the time to listen to the client and educate them on all of your offerings! Don't let that happen to you!

And…! You, yourself, have had this happen to you: a large company has spent thousands—sometimes millions—of dollars to get you to give them an opportunity to sell to you. One day, you find yourself in need of their product or service, you remember all those ads, and you head to their local storefront, walk in and…run right into the most rude, incompetent, downright off-putting counter person you've ever met. All of the money the parent company spent to get you to walk in in the first place had been torpedoed by a minimum wage clerk inside of seconds. Monitor your employees closely to insure this doesn't happen to your business!

Customer Service Is Marketing!

You read that right! And businesses who understand this concept are far and away ahead of their competition from the get go! So many companies believe that their responsibilities end with the sale…and they lose business because of it! How many times have you bought from a business for the first time only to run into problems? If you are like most folks, the first problem could be easily fixed. But the issue just gets worse and worse because no one is willing to step up and take care of the problem! Everyone has had (multiple) issues like this!

Let's face it…no one wants to deal with an unhappy customers. But more times that not, if you face the issue head on and take care of it immediately, you can turn an unhappy customer into a delighted one! Why? Because unfortunately people are used to terrible customer service. So when you step up and immediately take care of the problem (and offer them 10% off their next order) they are surprised and delighted! As I heard someone say the other day when discussing customer service, "Everyone can be a hero when things are going well!"

Example: A brand new coffee/wine bar opened in a town nearby. The response from around the community had been very positive. They were unique in the area and quickly developed a reputation for good customer service and a relaxing atmosphere.

After a short time, another local business person and his wife patronized the bar for the first time. His experience was terrible. The drinks were wrong. The food was slow. And the waiter was rude. Unfortunately it happens to many small businesses. Now the worst part…the customer left without voicing a complaint. Instead he left and told a group of friends about the bad experience. (Yes…that would be the worst case scenario).

Luckily one of the friends knew the bar owner and told him about the experience. The new bar owner acted immediately. He fired the waiter (he had had some small complaints before) and called the disgruntled customer to personally apologize. He welcomed them back and offered them a free drink and discounted appetizers simply for another chance!

Not only did the unhappy customer come back and become a regular…but they told this story of GREAT customer service again and again! Now that is great marketing!

And that is why Great Customer Service can often become one of your best marketing tools. Because that fantastic customer service can help you create the much sought after Word of Mouth advertising…and we all want that!

So when you are considering the marketing for your small business, make sure you take a truly big picture approach to the effort. Sometimes these easy (and yes, FREE) adjustments can make a BIG difference in your marketing and sale efforts! Remember that when it comes to marketing your business…everything matters!

Big Marketing in Tough Times

In recent years, we small business owners have seen some tough times. At the time of this book, the country is in the midst of a recession. And to be honest, many parts of the country have not been strong economically since before 9/11. In times like this, the first instinct of many small business owners is to cut their marketing way back...or out completely.

This is a huge mistake. As I once heard someone say, "Cutting out advertising to save money is like stopping your clock to save time." If you are not constantly marketing your business, you soon won't have a business to worry about!

During tough times, business owners are faced with tough decisions. Just be responsible...and wary of making drastic decisions when it comes to promoting your business. Now is the time to be even MORE targeted than ever before!

Increase Your Marketing...Increase Your Marketing Share
It may sound a bit crazy, but a down time is a great time to really increase your marketing presence! Most of your competitors will be looking for ways to scale back...and they will cut back their marketing. By increasing your marketing efforts, you can increase your marketing share during a tough time. And when the economy bounces back, you will be in a better position for real growth!

Don't believe me? Check out this study for proof!

DOES IT PAY TO ADVERTISE DURING A RECESSIONARY PERIOD?

In a study of U.S. recessions, McGraw-Hill Research analyzed 600 companies from 1980-1985. The results showed that business-to-business **Firms that Maintained or Increased their Advertising Expenditures** during the 1981-1982 recession Averaged **Significantly Higher Sales** growth, both during the recession and for the following three years, than those that eliminated or decreased advertising. By 1985, sales of companies that were **Aggressive Recession Advertisers had Risen 256%** over those that didn't keep up their advertising.

In addition, a series of six studies conducted by the research firm of Meldrum & Fewsmith showed conclusively that **Advertising Aggressively during Recessions not only Increases Sales but Increases Profits.** This fact has held true for all post-World War II recessions studied by The American Business Press starting in 1949.

So use this time of downturn to plant the seeds for future growth by increasing your marketing efforts.

Become More Targeted
Notice I said increase your marketing "efforts." I didn't say dollars. My entire marketing philosophy is about creating targeted efforts, and during a down time that targeted effort becomes even more imperative.

You need to make sure that each and every dollar you spend has an impact on your sales…and ultimately your bottom line. So now is a great time to re-examine the way you are spending your marketing dollars. If you need to cut something out, consider cutting the forms of advertising from which you don't see any return. These are often your "habit buys." The local school calls and asks you to run an ad in the yearbook. The local club asks you to sponsor a program. Things like this might cost $25, $50, or even $100 per time and probably don't really give you any return. If you are going to cut something…there's the place to start.

Now that you have trimmed some fat by eliminating ads that don't show returns, take that money and increase your efforts that DO generate success. By simply doing this one strategy, you will be pleasantly surprised by the return.

Create a Target List

Each business is different, but when you are re-evaluating your marketing efforts, I encourage folks to create a target list of customers they want to have. If you can't name specific potential customers, then create the image of what your ideal customer would look like. Doing so will help you to focus your efforts. What would it take to make this person or business (and lots more like them) a customer of mine? Once you have a clear vision of the type of person you want—and what it would take to get them—attack that plan!

Re-visit Dormant Accounts

When you are looking at ways to create new customers, you need to consider ways to get old customers back! Sometimes they have stopped doing business with your for legitimate reasons…but sometimes not. Now is a great time to reach out an olive branch to those customers that used to don your doorstep regularly…and see if you can get them back!

See the People

One of my early sales managers used to say that if you wanted to increase your sales, you needed to "see the people." With all of the advertising methods, venues, and options, we can all fall into the trap of waiting for customers to come to us. It's an easy trap to fall into so don't beat yourself up if you do it. But one of the best ways to jump start your sales is to simply go out and "see the people!"

Business is often built on relationships. And you can certainly strengthen these business relationships by showing your customers that you appreciate them. My advice would be to make these visits a "thank you" visit. Obviously you want to use these opportunities to sell yourself and your business. But you will be surprised by how much business will come to you when you show your customers that you care about them…and their business.

There's no doubt about it. Tough economic times are tough on small businesses. But by re-evaluating your marketing efforts, and making sure your efforts are more targeted, you can survive and position yourself for future growth!

On another note: these strategies are not only good when economic times are tough. They can be utilized anytime your business is in a rut! Re-read this chapter and get ready to hit the streets to increase your company's sales!

Steps to Recovery
1. Increase (or maintain) your marketing
2. Re-focus marketing to make sure it is targeted for best return
3. Create a target list of accounts
4. Re-visit dormant accounts
5. See the people
6. Say "Thank you!"

Be Targeted or Be Extinct!

Let me paint a picture.

A groggy man named Steve wipes the sleep from his eyes as he slowly puts his feet on the floor to begin a new day. He stumbles to the coffee maker to start his morning brew. After a quick shower, Steve looks into his closet and selects his favorite golf shirt, one given to him by a vendor. It's a nice name brand golf shirt with the vendor's logo on it…subtly on the sleeve.

After getting dressed Steve heads toward the coffee pot and selects his favorite mug. He has quite a few in the cupboard, but for whatever reason, he usually uses one of about three of them. As you might expect, the mug was given to him at the end of last year by an office supplies vendor. He makes a mental note that he needs to check his office stock of paper when he gets to work.

Carrying his favorite mug, Steve heads to his home office to check his email and check the news online. He heads opens his internet browser and it goes to his selected home page…his favorite site. Then he opens his email and quickly and finds an e-newsletter from a company from which he requested information. He quickly scans it and sees a link that catches his interest. He clicks on the link to get more information.

Finally Steve looks at his watch (a gift from his company) and realizes it's time to head to the office. He grabs his briefcase and folder, with his own company logo attached, and heads out the door. With the radio on his favorite pre-set, Steve makes the mad dash to work as painlessly as possible before beginning his work day.

So what's the point? The point is, in a not so subtle way, I have explained about a dozen ways to reach your **targeted** customer (in this case, Steve) before he even gets to work! And there are countless more opportunities with each demographic each day.

The fact is, most consumers are creatures of habit. They do the same routines (for the most part) every day. As I said in the example, Steve had a cupboard full of mugs, but he chose the same 3 just about every day. For one reason or another he had decided that these were his favorite. While some may think this is boring, it actually helps those of us that want to market to a specific target audience.

As a small business owner or marketer, we need to paint a picture of what that "perfect" customer would look like. What does he/she look like? What does he/she like to do? Where do they go? What are their ROUTINES? Once you have that information, you can design a targeted marketing campaign that can effectively reach them every single day!

And let me be clear. I believe this is your most powerful tool for business sustainability and growth. Businesses that continue to randomly try different marketing tools and sales tricks will inevitably fail. Because in this constantly changing world of marketing options, it is easy to lose sight of your vision…and your target customer!

You need to be targeted…or be extinct! If you have everyone as your customer, then you have no customers.

If you can, however, quickly identify your perfect customer—and you can picture their day—and create targeted ways to reach them, then you are ready for BIG growth. If you can consistently reach a higher percentage of real potential customers in the right place, then you will have a much higher chance of converting them to customers. Then it's just simple math!

Of course this assumes you have created a nice marketing image, a clearly defined USP, and a great service or product. But we would not be at this point in the book if you had not achieved that, right? If you don't know what I am talking about, head back to the beginning of this book and start over!

But at the end of the day, we small business owners want to get as much return as possible on each dollar we spend. This ROI (Return On Investment) is imperative for operating a successful and profitable business. In order to maintain this high ROI, we need to target, target, target.

Good luck. And get out there and **Think Big** for your Small Business!